Building a Winner

By

Marcie Aboff

Illustrations by
Molly Delaney

CELEBRATION PRESS
Pearson Learning Group

Contents

CHAPTER 1

The Contest

"It's here!" Kyle Miller yelled when he opened his mailbox. "It's here!"

Usually the mail was for his mom or dad. Sometimes there was a birthday party invitation for him or for his younger brother, Justin. Today, though, Kyle had received the latest issue of *Linx Magazine*.

Kyle sat down in the kitchen and eagerly flipped through the magazine. There were pictures of new Linx sets, a Linx calendar, and even Linx comics. Kyle loved building with Linx, colorful plastic pieces that linked together. Kyle had built castles, spaceships, and even a soccer stadium, all made out of Linx.

Suddenly Kyle stopped flipping. His eyes stopped on one page. He read:

CONTEST!
Create Your Own Original Linx Model.
Judges coming to your local area soon!

Kyle quickly looked down the list of locations. When he saw the Hillside Community Center listed, Kyle's heart beat faster. Hillside was the next town over!

Kyle thought hard. Then he snapped his fingers and hurried into the playroom. He had an idea.

Kyle's brother, Justin, was zooming cars around his racetrack. Kyle wasn't interested in that. He took out all of his Linx models and started pulling them apart.

"What are you doing?" Justin asked.

"I'm entering the Linx contest," Kyle exclaimed. "I'm going to build the greatest Linx robot ever!"

"Can I help?" Justin asked.

"Sure," Kyle said, "but here's what I want the robot to look like." Kyle drew a picture and showed it to Justin.

"Cool!" said Justin. "I can do that."

First Kyle separated all of his Linx pieces.
He grouped all the rods with the rods, all the
wheels with the wheels, and all the connectors
with the connectors. Then he started
separating the Linx pieces by color, too.

"Let's just build the robot already!" Justin
said. "All this sorting will take forever!"

"We have to get organized first," Kyle said. "It will save time later."

Kyle and Justin heard the doorbell ring. A few seconds later, Kyle's friend Rosa walked into the playroom.

"Hey, guys," she said. "What are you doing?"

"We're building a robot!" Justin said. "Galaxa the Great!"

"*Galaxa*?" Kyle asked doubtfully. Then he saw Justin's hopeful face. "All right, all right. It's a good name," he admitted.

While Kyle showed Rosa his drawing, Justin told Rosa about the contest. "We're going to win!" Justin said.

"Can I help, too?" Rosa asked.

"Sure!" Kyle said.

"I'll bring the Linx sets from my house," Rosa said. "I'll be right back!" Rosa ran out of the house, slamming the door behind her.

When Rosa came back, she was carrying a big plastic box. She opened it and dumped an assortment of Linx pieces onto the table.

"Great!" Kyle said. "This will help make Galaxa even bigger! Let's get going!"

The next day at school, while Mrs. Carson was grading papers, Rosa leaned over to Kyle.

"My dad said he'd drive us to the Linx contest," she whispered.

Kyle smiled and gave Rosa the thumbs up sign. "Sounds good," he whispered back.

Then Kyle saw Brenda Foster reach into her desk and pull out *Linx Magazine*. She turned to Kyle and Rosa.

"What are *you* two making for the Linx contest?" Brenda asked.

Rosa looked down at her desk. She thought Brenda was too nosy.

Kyle didn't say anything, either.

"Kyle Miller!" Brenda said so loudly that Mrs. Carson looked up. Brenda lowered her voice. "I'm talking to you! I'm entering the contest, too, with Philip Lee. We're making something *really* special."

Kyle still didn't say anything. He looked at Philip. Kyle knew Philip had more Linx pieces than anyone. His bedroom was practically a Linx toy store!

Mrs. Carson told the students to open their math books so Kyle reached into his desk and pulled out his book. He had a hard time concentrating on fractions, though. Kyle kept thinking about Galaxa and the Linx contest. He hadn't thought about the competition he might have. What if Philip and Brenda won, instead of his own team?

CHAPTER 3

It's a Secret

Each day after school that week, Kyle, Justin, and Rosa worked on building Galaxa. Sometimes the Linx pieces didn't move smoothly enough, and they had to use a different-sized connector. Other times they would come up with a new idea. Then they had to revise their building plan and start over.

In the schoolyard one morning, Rosa
noticed Brenda and Philip huddled together.
They were looking at *Linx Magazine*. Philip
was writing something down on a piece of
paper. Rosa knew they must be talking about
their Linx model, whatever it was.

   "Brenda and Philip are always together," Rosa said to Kyle. "I wonder what they're making."

   Kyle didn't want to admit it, but he was curious, too. "Don't worry," he said. "Galaxa will be excellent. When we finish his arms, he'll be able to move his hands and hold things."

Rosa walked by Brenda and Philip. When Philip saw her, he hid the paper behind his back.

Brenda smiled. "I bet you want to know what *we're* making," she told Rosa.

"It's top-secret," Philip added.

"That's okay," Rosa said. "I guess we'll both find out at the judging this Saturday."

Competition

After school, Rosa hurried straight to Kyle's house to get to work. There were only a few more days to go, and they still needed to finish Galaxa's head.

All of a sudden, Justin burst into the playroom, looking pleased with himself.

"I know what they're building! I know what they're building!" Justin yelled.

"What are you talking about?" Kyle asked.

"Brenda and Philip's Linx model!" Justin said. "I know what it is!"

"So tell us!" Rosa demanded.

"Brenda's brother Jeremy is in my class,"
Justin told them breathlessly. "He told me
they're building an amusement park. It has a
roller coaster and a Ferris wheel that spins!"

Kyle and Rosa looked at each other.

"It can't be better than Galaxa the Great,"
Kyle said confidently.

Just then the doorbell rang. Kyle heard his mother talking in the hallway.

"Kyle," she called into the playroom. "You have company. Brenda and Philip are here."

Rosa and Justin jumped up and bolted out of the playroom. They slammed the door behind them.

"All right," Brenda said, marching toward Rosa and Justin. "I know my brother Jeremy ratted on us."

"Yeah," Philip said. "You know what we're building. Now we want to know what you're building!"

"It's a secret," Justin said.

Just then Kyle opened the playroom door and came out, quickly closing the door behind him.

"You can see it on one condition," Kyle said. Everyone stared at him. "If we show you our model, then we have to go to Brenda's house and see your amusement park," Kyle said firmly.

Brenda and Philip looked at each other. "It's a deal," Brenda said.

They all walked into the playroom.

"Wow, it's so big!" Philip said, staring at Galaxa.

"Look at what he can do!" Rosa said. She showed Brenda and Philip how Galaxa walked and moved his arms. His head also spun around, and he had a secret compartment in his stomach.

Brenda's eyes were large and wide. "Your robot is so cool!" she said.

The Secret's Out

When they got to Brenda's house and saw the amusement park, Kyle was pretty amazed, too. It had a Ferris wheel, a roller coaster, a swing ride, and even a food stand.

"Your park is really awesome!" Rosa said.

Brenda smiled. "Thanks. We used almost every Linx piece we had."

"Yeah," Philip added. "We wanted to make
the Ferris wheel really high in the middle of the
park, but then we didn't have enough pieces for
the roller coaster. We really wanted the park to
have a roller coaster and a slide, too."

"It is good," Brenda said carefully, "but I still
think something's missing."

The Ferris wheel had little Linx people sitting in the seats, and it spun around. Kyle stared at the set and turned the Ferris wheel around and around.

"I agree," Kyle finally said. "I think the park would look even better with a really gigantic ride in the middle."

"We only have a few pieces left," Brenda said. "We don't have enough to build another ride."

"Maybe not," Kyle said, "but I have an idea that might work out for all of us."

Everyone turned to look at Kyle. They all wondered what his idea could be.

The Judges Decide

Kyle woke up early Saturday morning. It was the day of the Linx judging. He and Justin wolfed down their breakfast. They were eager to get to the contest early.

When Rosa's father pulled up to their house, the kids piled into his van. Kyle's mom and dad followed in their car. Soon they all arrived at the community center.

There was a big crowd of kids and adults at
the community center—and so many Linx
models! Kyle walked past spaceships, castles,
and train sets. One model spelled out the
words "Linx Rules" in Linx pieces.

The Linx judges walked up and down the
aisles examining all the models.

Then they came to Galaxa. "What do you call this model?" one judge asked.

"Galaxa Amusement Park!" Kyle, Justin, Rosa, Brenda, and Philip all said together.

The judges nodded. They carefully examined the park, especially the huge Galaxa ride in the middle of it.

Galaxa the Great towered in the middle of the park. His outstretched arms had little seats hung on them. Linx people sat on the seats as Galaxa moved them up and down.

"Hmm," another judge said, examining the park. "That's very interesting." The judges wrote some notes on their pads and walked on to the next model.

The kids frowned. "He didn't seem too excited," Rosa said.

"Don't worry," Kyle's mom said. "Why don't we all get something to drink?" The children straggled slowly over to the food stand.

"It was fun building Galaxa Amusement Park together," Kyle said. "Even if we don't win," he added softly.

Brenda nodded. "Yeah, and I still think our Galaxa Amusement Park is *really* special. It has a giant robot and rides, and the giant robot even *is* a ride."

"We've made our decision," a judge announced over the microphone. Everyone rushed over to the judge's stand.

"All of the models were very creative and original," the judge said, "but we have chosen our winners." Then they announced the third-place winner, a submarine, and the second-place winner, a castle.

"And our first-place winner is . . .Galaxa Amusement Park!"

Kyle and the others jumped up and down. They cheered. Kyle put his arms around his friends. He already knew that Galaxa was great, and he agreed that the amusement park was special, but linking them together was what truly made them the best!